Prayer Book
for
Widows

Prayer Book for Widows

Kay M. Cozad

Our Sunday Visitor Publishing Division
Our Sunday Visitor, Inc.
Huntington, Indiana 46750

Nihil Obstat: Rev. Michael Heintz
Censor Librorum

Imprimatur: + John M. D'Arcy
Bishop of Fort Wayne-South Bend
December 29, 2003

Our Sunday Visitor Publishing Division
Our Sunday Visitor, Inc.
200 Noll Plaza
Huntington, IN 46750

ISBN: 1-59276-145-3 (Inventory No. T196)
LCCN: 2003113162

Cover design by Monica Haneline
Cover and interior art by Getty Images, Inc., copyright © 2002,
all rights reserved
Interior design by Sherri L. Hoffman

PRINTED IN THE UNITED STATES OF AMERICA

*In loving memory of my husband, Trent.
And for my earth angels, Sara and Emily,
and all my Joy and Hope friends.*

Contents

Introduction

The Lord is near to the brokenhearted,
and saves the crushed in spirit.
— PSALM 34:18

I believe that prayer is a necessity of life for people of faith. It is a gift from God for our own sake. He gives us this avenue to express our gratitude, to confess our shortcomings, to make our needs known, and to mightily praise His name. Prayer keeps the soul united with its Creator. It gives voice to the joys and sorrows of this life.

Prayer is an essential part of the Church community as well. It is the chain that links us together with God. And as God holds a special place in His heart for the widow, as evidenced in Scripture, so does His Church. He has held His Church accountable for the widows in its midst through the ages, and the Church has stood willing to honor them in their time of need. James 1:27 says, "Religion that is pure and undefiled before God and the Father, is this: to visit orphans and widows in their affliction, and to keep oneself unstained from the world." This rich tradition of my faith and prayer has brought me hope. So, with the Church, I aspire to honor the widow and bring her hope in her affliction with these prayers.

This book of prayers was born out of my own need to express myself to God on a heart level. These prayers give voice to the wanderings of my own personal grief journey.

Following the death of my husband, I was forced to begin a life that I could never have imagined or ever asked for. My faith was in God and His mercy, yet there were many times I felt so bereaved that I had no voice to express the pain I felt. No prayer came to unite me with God and keep me in His comforting presence. As I traveled the path of grief, in God's time and with His healing power, I began to write these prayers. I share them with you now — you who have lost your husband and are suffering the pain and confusion of loss.

Though we can acquaint ourselves with the logical stages of grief, we who experience loss know it is a journey of the heart. So, my hope is that if you find yourself, as I did, without strength to give voice to your need, this prayer book will be a starting place to find that voice.

May these words of prayer be helpful to you as you wander on your journey. I believe that the Lord knows our hearts, and that we feel His loving presence when we stay close to Him in prayer. Pray and take courage. Do the work of grief. May you find comfort and lasting peace as you travel this heart journey. And may the Lord turn your mourning into joy.

— KAY COZAD

CHAPTER ONE

You Have Met Death

*Even though I walk through the
valley of the shadow of death,
I fear no evil; for thou art with me;
thy rod and thy staff, they comfort me.*
— PSALM 23:4

ou have met death. You have lost someone very dear — your husband, your other half. The void he left in your life is gaping. The pain and sadness you experience is intense. This is the beginning of a long and difficult journey: the journey through grief. Though others have traveled this path before you, your journey will be distinctly your own. Honor it with prayerful faith and hope, one step at a time.

The following prayers are cries of anguish to Our Lord. Use them as a starting point from which to pour out your soul. Myriad emotions will flow in like the tide as you struggle with your loss. Give them all to God. He desires your alliance as He shoulders your pain. He is ever-loving and faithful, and He will answer your prayer.

YOU KNOW MY PAIN

Lord,
You have called my husband home.
He is gone from me.
I have lost half of myself.
Where do I go from here?
How do I survive?

I turn to You now.
You know my pain.

I am exhausted by grief.
Waves of emotion flood over me.

Carry me, please.
Have mercy on me and light my way.
Bring me comfort in my sadness.
Sustain me as I set about the task
of living life without my husband.
Gather my broken heart in Your love
and help me get through today.
Amen.

MY HUSBAND

Heavenly Father,
I bring to You my hope
that You have welcomed my dear one
into Your heavenly kingdom.
Embrace him in Your loving arms.
Grant him eternal rest, Lord.

He was my husband and my friend.
A good and faithful servant.

As I take in the unfamiliar, knowing that
    he is gone,
I pray that he is well.

His death has left a painful void in my life.
But I believe he fills his place with You.

Father, please give him my love as I await
    the time
when we will be together again.
And know that I am grateful
for the peace that he enjoys with You now.
Amen.

CHAPTER TWO

The Funeral

*Yea, thou art my rock
and my fortress;
for thy name's sake
lead me and guide me.*
— PSALM 31:3

isbelief and denial may be the overwhelming emotions you feel after learning of your loved one's death. Numbness may befall you. But custom calls you to action. You must arrange your beloved husband's funeral service. There is so much to attend to in preparation for honoring him. Here are prayers expressing the need for God's own strength and guidance during this whirlwind and arduous process.

GUIDE MY CHOICE

Lord,
Is this really happening?
Is my husband really gone?
The task set before me
is the most horrific I have ever had to face.
I feel frantic and at the same time
totally numb.

Please, please, be with me now
as I prepare his funeral.
Guide me to make right choices
in my desire to honor him.
Bless the people who will offer
direction in my choices.
Grant me the wisdom to arrange
this memorial according to Your will.

Thank you for holding my dear one,
now that I cannot.
Amen.

GIVE ME STRENGTH

Father,
I come before You, weeping and wailing.
My beloved husband is dead.
The weight of my sadness shrouds my soul.
Why did this happen?
What will I do?

I feel . . .
    numb,
    scared,
    sick,
    confused,
    exhausted,
    desperate,
    forgetful,
    unbelieving,
    sad,
    clumsy,
    angry. . . .

These conflicting emotions drain me of all
    my strength.
Please be my strength, O Lord.
Remind me that Your strength comes in many
    different forms.
Open my heart to my family and friends.
My hope is in You.
Amen.

COMFORT MY VIEW

O Lord,
My mind is restless.
My soul is weary.
Never have I known such despair.

Please sustain me now as I prepare to
host my husband's memorial visitation.

So many loved him and will honor him
    this day
Give me strength to welcome them
and to share words of sympathy and comfort.

As we come together to remember my beloved
    husband
with stories and prayers,
help us embrace the tears as well as the laughter.
I know he would welcome both.

Work through each of us to bring comfort to our
    heavy hearts.
Grant us peace in our mourning and faith in Your
    promise
that You have embraced him in Your kingdom
    forever.
Amen.

STRENGTH FOR THE FUNERAL

Lord,
These past days since my husband died have been a
    hazy blur.
Today I prepare for his funeral service and burial.
Family and friends surround me, yet I feel
    so alone.
The finality of this day frightens me so.
But I take special care in grooming myself
    to honor my beloved.
Oh, the dread I feel weighs heavy on my heart.

Strengthen me now, Lord, as I prepare
    to honor my husband
and remember his precious life.
May this honoring bring comfort to my soul
and glory to Your name.

In confidence I pray that all who remember my
    beloved today
will share in Your peace and know of Your promise
    of everlasting life.
Amen.

CHAPTER THREE

The Days After

*For my life is spent with sorrow,
and my years with sighing;
my strength fails because of my misery,
and my bones waste away.*

— PSALM 31:10

The funeral is now over. Everyone has returned home. You are left to survive — alone. Your life has changed forever, yet you must go on. As the numbness lifts, pain and sadness sometimes make it difficult to find a routine in daily living. Your health may be at risk. The Father desires your well-being. He knows what you need. Use the following prayers for His divine assistance with your health issues.

PEACEFUL SLEEP

Father of comfort,
hear me now as I lie down to sleep.
I feel exhausted from the work of grief.
Yet, I cannot sleep.
My mind races with the worries of the day.
Grief steals my peace like a thief in the night.
Grant me the grace to quiet my mind and give my
    body rest.

As I climb into my bed, it seems so vast
    and empty.
I miss my husband. How I long for his embrace.
These lonely hours bring me no repose.
Despair threatens to consume me.
Grant me the hope that Your love will sustain me
in the dark and lonely night.

Please, Lord, lay Your hand of healing peace upon
  my restless soul.
Grant me peaceful sleep as the night moves slowly
  on.
May I rest until the morning light
and arise to begin again to glorify Your name.
Amen.

MY PHYSICAL WELL-BEING

Lord,
I pray for my physical well-being this day
and the will to attain it.
In my grief, fatigue has overwhelmed me.

Exercise has kept me fit.
But now I find it difficult to put one foot in front
  of the other.
Please, Lord, give me the strength to do
one activity that will cause my blood to flow.
Be my energy.

Grief has robbed me of my appetite as well.
Food holds no flavor for me now.
Help me to eat nutritious foods throughout the day.
Be my sustenance.

I believe my body is Your temple.
I must not neglect it now.

So hold me up in my lethargy
and inspire me to care for my physical needs.
In this way, may I glory in Your peace and well-being.
Amen.

PATIENCE, PATIENCE, PATIENCE

O God!
I find myself impatient in this life I now must lead.
Each day holds little things that irritate and frustrate
    me.
And, Lord, the things that people say!

I cry out to You now,
in my frustration and my pain.
Please grant me tolerance amidst the hurt.
Help me persevere when things seem out of hand.

So much has changed in this life of mine,
yet the sameness of my grief gnaws at my soul.
Help me move on, in Your time and at Your pace.
Give me patience with others and with myself
as You heal my broken heart.
Amen.

LIFT ME FROM DEPRESSION

Dear Lord,
as time passes, a violent sea of emotion tosses me
    about.
Living without my beloved husband is confusing
    and difficult work.
I am swept to a dark and lonely place.
Deep sadness and disarming lethargy engulf my
    days.
Despair is waiting on the shore.

O God! I miss my mate!
I ache for his return.
I cannot find the energy for this day.
I am drowning!
I am drowning!

You, Lord, are all I have.
Nothing else matters to me now.
Lift me gently, Lord.
Piece together my broken heart.
Help me find meaning in this life once again.
Grant me a grateful heart.

I call to You, Lord, my rescuer!
Lift me from this sea of darkness.
Let not these waves of sadness

and despair devour me.
Extend Your grace that I may work through this
    depression
and find life and joy again.
Amen.

YOUR STRENGTH IN MY PAIN

O Lord,
I miss my husband and my old life so terribly
that my heart aches!
The pain of my loss is almost unbearable.
How many more tears must I shed?
It seems that's all I do.

Life holds little comfort for me, Lord.
This grief I feel is so intense.
I seek peace in Your presence.
Help me work through this pain,
moment by moment.
Please heal my shattered heart.
You have promised that in my weakness You are
    strong.
Be my strength as I put my hope in You.
Amen.

MY CHILDREN

Bless my children, Lord,
as they mourn the loss
of the one who was their father.
My heart aches for them.

We mourn together cautiously,
wanting to soothe, not to upset.

Embody in me Your love and compassion
that I may counsel my children as they grieve.
Show me how to comfort them
and to be mindful of what they need.
And grant me the grace to accept their love
as they share their loss with me.

In this time of deep distress, be merciful, Lord.
Give us the grace to grow closer to You
and closer as a family.
May we all remember Your promise of eternal life
and Your constant, healing love.
Amen.

CHAPTER FOUR

Change

"For I know the plans I have
for you, says the Lord,
plans for welfare and not for evil,
to give you a future and a hope."
— JEREMIAH 29:11

As time passes, so much in your life changes. As you work through your grief, you are faced with readjusting your perspective on life. When is it time to clean out his things? How do you let him go? Travel, worship, and even dinnertime are not untouched by your loss. Perhaps you must return to work or sell your home. You may begin to wonder who you really are and what your role is in life, now that you are alone. This difficult part of the grief journey may require introspection. God will provide for your needs if you ask in prayer.

CHANGING LIFE, UNCHANGING LOVE

Heavenly Father,
You are my source of enduring love
in this changing sea of life.
My life has changed in every way
since the day my husband died.

Lord, be my unchanging source of . . .
    comfort, when the sadness overwhelms me.
    presence, when I sit in loneliness.
    forgiveness, when envy clouds my soul.
    calm, when anger burns inside.
    peace, when chaos surrounds me.

tolerance, when I feel hurt.
wisdom, when I am confused.
purpose, when I can't get out of bed.
acceptance, when I fight against this life.

I pray to know Your merciful and constant care.
Keep me strong in faith and hope
as I live on in this ever-changing world.
Amen.

WHO AM I?

Father,
who am I without my husband?
He was my life partner, my anchor, and my safety
    net.
I feel I lost my identity when I lost him.

Who am I?
All my hopes and dreams for our future
died along with him.
I am fearful of what awaits me.
In this couples world, I am reminded that I am
    alone.
Let not my anger and resentment cloud my mind
when I must make decisions on my own.
I feel ill-equipped to do my work and his as well.
What will become of me?

Lord, as I try to adjust to living without his presence,
help me keep his memory in my heart.
As I discover who I am now,
give me the time I need to mourn my losses.
Reveal to me Your purpose for my life.
Work in me the miracle of Your healing,
that I may find myself and have lasting joy in life
    again.
Amen.

YOUR PRESENCE IN MY LONELINESS

Lord,
I used to feel You in the gentle breeze that
    whispered past my cheek.
I'd see You in my beloved's eyes as he gazed across
    the room.
I'd hear You in the melody of the robin welcoming
    the dawn.

But now my grief and loneliness cloud my senses.
I cannot see You, Lord!
When in a crowd of people, I feel so alone!
My only companion is the ache of loneliness.
I miss my husband so!
He has left an empty place in my heart and in my
    home.
I fear the silence will swallow me.

Lord, I pray, make Your presence known to me
    again.
Clear my senses that I may honor You,
and fill that empty place.
Grant me peace in Your presence.
Bless my loneliness, and be that gentle breeze
that brings me closer to You.
Amen.

LETTING GO

O Lord,
My husband's presence surrounds me as I look upon
    his worldly possessions.
Each treasure brings a loving memory to mind.
Now some tell me it's time to clean out.
They say it will help me forget.
I never want to forget the man I loved
and shared my life with.
How do I let his things go, Lord?

I trust that in Your time
You will nudge me toward letting go.
Remind me that letting go is not forgetting.
And that it happens over time.
And when You do, Lord,
give me the grace to follow through.

And when his things have all been shared,
I will cherish what I will keep.
I will let him go, Lord, but let his sweet memory
    live on.
So with a sad and grateful heart I say, "Amen."

My Faith, My Church

O God,
I find it difficult to come to church
without my beloved husband.
I sit in silence, feeling all alone,
and I am crippled by the pain of grief.
Emotions well up inside me as I see couples gather
    here.
I find it hard to pray.
I am so angry that You allowed my beloved to die!
Why, Lord, why?

Sustain me now as my faith wavers.
Inspire me in this place of worship
that I may find Your peace.
Shower Your mercy on my troubled soul.
And grant me hope in the promise of everlasting
    life.
Amen.

GUIDE ME IN FINANCE

O Father,
so much has happened
since my dear one died.
I have been left to make decisions on my own.
Sometimes I feel so overwhelmed
by legal and financial decisions to be made.
I no longer have him as my partner and confidant.
I feel so burdened and all alone.

I will do nothing without a prayer
for wisdom and confidence.
Direct my thinking, and send me
good, honest people who will advise me well.
I thank You for sharing this burden, Lord,
for You are my mighty counselor.
Amen.

MOVING

Heavenly Father,
the decision has been made.
I must move.
I am saddened to be leaving this house
where we made so many memories.
But with Your guiding hand I will move on.

Packing up and letting go are daunting tasks for me.
I pray for the strength to face my grief
as I work to move my things.

So on this moving day,
I leave this house in Your hands,
and I ask Your blessing
on those who come to make their own memories
    here.

I trust that You will go before me
and bless my new abode.
May Your spirit reside with me in this new place.
Bless friends and family with
love and laughter when they enter here.
May I live in harmony with my new neighbors.
And as You shelter me in my grief,
please make this house a home.
Amen.

SHARE MY TABLE

As I sit down to my evening meal,
I am grateful for Your bounty.
But, Lord, I have no desire to eat here all alone.

Memories of a happier time
when I shared meals with my husband

fill my heart with sadness and my soul with
    loneliness.
We enjoyed our food together
as we explored and shared our day.

But now, Lord, that You have called him home,
I am left to eat alone.
So I invite You to share my table
and to be present with me now.
Bless the silence and this food
as it nourishes my body.
You are the bread of everlasting life.
Be the nourishment for my soul.
Amen.

TRAVEL WITH ME, LORD

Be behind me, Lord.
My lonely heart is not in this.
I pray that You will give me
the desire to travel on alone.

Go before me, Lord.
Map out my course.
Fill me with courage as I plan this trek alone.

Travel with me, Lord.
Be the light on my way.
Open my heart to this expedition

and all that it may bring.
Let me not shrink with fear or sadness
as I journey on alone.

Bring me home safely, Lord.
Give me a grateful heart,
for You are with me always
and everywhere I go.
Amen.

BACK TO WORK

Father,
they say enough time has passed for me to grieve.
They say it's time to be over his death and get back
    to normal life.
I don't feel "over it," Lord.
Sometimes the waves of grief wash over me at such
    unexpected times.
I feel so overwhelmed.

But I must return to work.
My interest and desire for the work I do is gone,
for I am exhausted with the work of grief.

I turn to You, Lord, that in my grief You will give
    me strength.
Increase in me a spirit of energy and motivation,
that I might do my job in the best way possible.

Help me to be pleasant to my co-workers
and open to their questions and support.
Give me clarity, that I may focus on my task.
Grant me compassion for myself when sadness
     interrupts my pace
— and the strength to return to it.
Give me balance between work and rest,
that I may not use my job to escape the work of
     grief.

I work for You today, Lord, in the hope that my
     interest will one day return.
Until that day I pray that I may endure this loss
     with healing grace and dignity.
Amen.

GETTING ON WITH GRIEF

Heavenly Father,
as I slow down,
the loneliness creeps in.
I find myself alone.
I've kept busy since my beloved died.
It seemed easier that way.

But now as I rest in quiet,
the pain of grief steals over me.
How I miss him and our old life!

My heart aches for his embrace!
Give me the will to face this pain
and Your love to heal my heart.

You've helped me see that my busyness has kept my
    grief at bay.
Now as I begin to face it, I need Your grace much
    more.
I know now that the only way back to life is
    through the pain of grief.
Lord, please hold my fragile emotions in Your
    tender hands.
Stay with me and direct my steps on this journey of
    the heart.
Amen.

CHAPTER FIVE

Special Days

*Set your minds on things that are above,
not on things that are on earth.*
— COLOSSIANS 3:2

*As the weeks and months pass, special dates reap-
pear that mark your life — dates that in the past
have been times of celebration and ceremony. Birthdays,
anniversaries, and holidays are all meaningful days
when shared with a loved one. Now that your husband
has died, these important dates may bring a sense of
dread. Being prepared for an anticipation reaction days
before the date is important. Use the prayers in this
chapter to connect with the Father as He blesses these
dates and comforts you through them.*

HIS BIRTHDAY PRAYER

Birthdays are for celebrating.
Some regret the coming of each year.
But, oh, to have the chance to celebrate this day
once more with my beloved spouse.
For now I have only memories of the passing of the
    years.

Father,
in the days before his birthday
fond memories are bittersweet.
His absence leaves me empty and reminds me of my
    loss.
How will I fill his day?

I pray, Lord, sustain me with Your grace,
and grant me faith that he is celebrating with You in
eternal love.
Give me the heart to remember him on his day
and to celebrate his life.
Amen.

MY BIRTHDAY PRAYER

Lord, it's my birthday.
You created me.
You know my comings and goings.
I should want to celebrate my life.
But today I feel so alone.
My heart is heavy, and I feel so sad.
I miss my husband's loving presence.
Help me, Lord.

I am grateful for family and friends who acknowledge
me this day.
Though the place my husband held is empty,
their love will sustain me.
For I find no joy in this day.

Please grant me the spirit of jubilance
for Your loving presence in my life.
For I walk alone in sadness on my birthday.
Amen.

OUR WEDDING ANNIVERSARY

Dear Father,
As the anniversary of our wedding draws near,
I pray that You hold my husband in Your gentle
    embrace.
Share with him the endless joy of knowing You.
Shower him with Your love and grace.
Remind him, if it be Your will, of my undying love
    for him.

These days are sometimes hard for me,
as memories of our sweet vows
wring my heart and tears flow silently.
As I walk this earth alone,
I ask You, please, for grace.
Give me courage, Lord, for in my weakness You are
    strong.
I have placed my faith in You.

O Lord, I pray that on the day my journey ends,
and I come home to You,
that my beloved be there waiting, too.
Reunite us for all eternity in Your everlasting love.
Until then, I wait in hopeful faith and pray to You.
Amen.

THE FIRST ANNIVERSARY

O Lord,
be with me today on the first anniversary of my
    husband's death.
The anticipation of the coming of this day has
    nearly drained me.
Has it already been a year? It seems like yesterday.
I have felt as if life were settling around me as I
    journey on alone.
Yet, it has all come back to me once again.
I find myself in tears, and I am clumsy and forlorn.

I come to You on bended knee.
I seek Your lasting peace.
Grant me sweet memories of the past
to comfort my quaking soul,
and replenish my hope for Your vision of the
    future.

Thank you, Lord, for Your presence in my family
    and friends.
Knowing they remember him lifts my heart.
As I remember the events of that tragic day,
turn my thoughts to ones of hope.
Help me weather this critical day with Your comfort
    and grace.

Bring me safely to another day and turn my
    mourning into joy.
Amen.

MILESTONES

Dear Lord,
so many special dates and events
mark time spent without my beloved.
Today is another important day, a milestone without
    him.
As I grieve the loss of this dear man,
and what could have been this day,
I ask You to console me with Your everlasting love.

Though I believe he is here with us in spirit,
I am heartbroken that we are unable to share this
    day in flesh.
His empty place speaks forever of our loss.
My heart rushes from anger to sadness and back
    again.

The memories of days gone and thoughts of events
    to come
bring tears to bear again.
Please grant me peace,
that I may celebrate Your goodness in this day.
Amen.

THANKSGIVING

Heavenly Father,
It is harvest time, when we turn to You in gratitude
    for Your bounty;
a day of thanksgiving as family gathers around the
    table
for a traditional turkey dinner with thoughts of all
    the blessings
You have bestowed.

I, too, have many blessings to be thankful for.
Yet my prayer of thanks rings hollow in me, Lord.
The blessings of my husband and my life with him
    are gone.
There is a sadness as I look upon his empty chair.

Father, I am grateful for having known my beloved
    husband.
But You know the emptiness I feel now.
In Your bountiful goodness, fill me with Your
    healing grace.
Grant me a sincere and grateful heart as I praise
    Your name today.
Amen.

THE CHRISTMAS PRAYER

The Christmas season is upon us.
A time to celebrate our Savior's birth.
A time of illumination and love,
and of gathering with loved ones.

Forgive me, Lord, but my heart is heavy.
Memories of past Christmas times spent in laughter
    and love
bring an emptiness to me now.

Comfort me in my loneliness.
Be my light as I share in this sacred season.
Quiet my sorrowful heart.

As my husband celebrates with the angels,
open my eyes so I may see the joy that this season
    brings.
Help me to keep my heart centered on You,
for Your birth brought us resurrection and new life.
Sustain me with Your peace.
Amen.

EASTER

Risen Lord,
I look around and see all the signs of spring.
New life bursts forth in the colors of the flowers and
the birds in the trees.
Yet inside my heart there is darkness and despair.
For the loss of my husband is so difficult to bear.

I know You love me, Lord, because You died for me.
Let Easter and the celebration of Your resurrection
bring light to my darkness.
Lead me on this sad and lonely path to new life.
You, Lord, are my saving grace.
Fill me with the hope of being reunited with my
beloved husband one day.
For I cling to Your promise of eternal life.
Amen.

CHAPTER SIX

For Those Who Care

> *Blessed be the God and Father of*
> *our Lord Jesus Christ, the Father of mercies*
> *and God of all comfort, who comforts us*
> *in all our affliction, so that we may be*
> *able to comfort those who are in any*
> *affliction, with the comfort with which*
> *we ourselves are comforted by God.*
> — 2 CORINTHIANS 1:3-4

There are many people behind the scenes who love you and want to find a way to help during your time of intense grief. Those who wish to help may be at a loss as to what to do. Prayer is always a good way to help. This chapter was written with those compassionate hearts in mind. The following prayers are for caregivers as they comfort the grieving soul.

How Can I Help?

Heavenly Father,
I lift _____ up in prayer,
as she mourns her husband's death.
She seems so fragile and alone.
Her life will never be the same.

As I lift her up to You,
direct my actions, Lord,
that I may be present to her when she needs
    someone near.
Open my ears that I may listen with compassion
    and acceptance.
And give me words of comfort for her sad and
    broken heart.

Be present to her in peace and strength,
and whisper Your promise of everlasting life.

I thank You for Your grace.
Amen.

STRENGTH AS I GRIEVE, TOO

Lord,
I come to You with a troubled heart.
I am torn in two.
While I grieve the loss of my loved one,
I desire to comfort _____.
My loss is great.
But she has lost her spouse.
How devastating that must be.

Give me the compassion and the energy to reach
   out to her now.
Use me, Lord, to comfort her in any way You
   choose.
I humbly ask that as You do, You may also comfort
   me.
With a grateful but grieving heart I say, "Amen."

WIDOW TO WIDOW

Heavenly Father,
I continue on this grief journey since my beloved
    died.
I am grateful that You have been my constant
    companion.
Now my friend has lost her spouse.
I feel deep sorrow for her.
I have become awash in memories
of my own as my heart is torn anew.

Help me, Lord, to be present to my grieving friend,
for I am familiar with this dark journey she has
    begun.
Though my pain is still fresh for me,
please give me the heart
to reach out to her and take her hand.
Help me to give her hope.
I lift her and all widows up in their loneliness and
    pain.
Bless us all with faith, hope, and tender mercy.
Amen.

CHAPTER SEVEN

From Mourning to Joy

*"I will turn their mourning into joy,
I will comfort them, and
give them gladness for sorrow."*
JEREMIAH 31:13

There comes a time, as you do the work of grief, when you begin to notice joy in your life. It comes unexpectedly at first — in small doses. But eventually, you find happiness more often, and gratitude begins to reshape your heart. You discover that God has carried you through the pain and has directed your steps all along this lonesome path. There is much to be thankful for. The following prayers will remind you of your faithful God, who has turned your mourning into joy.

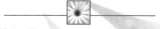

FOR FAMILY AND FRIENDS

Blessings on my circle of shelter,
my family and friends.
All, in their own way, have brought me comfort and
    hope
during this dark and painful time.
Their generosity and compassion surround me.
You have blessed me richly
with these loving people.
They have come to call,
and they have listened,
comforted, and grieved.
As they offer me their gift of self,
please bless them richly in return.
Amen.

MY HUSBAND'S LIFE

I sing praises to You, Lord,
for my husband's life.
He was a gift beyond compare.
His presence lit up a room.
He loved me and was my safety net.

He was whimsical and witty,
strong and handy to have around.
He was kind and intelligent.
He loved and served You, Lord,
and his fellow man.

He was diligent at work, but with a gentle hand.
He loved his family and his friends.
He treasured time spent with them.

Oh, I cherish my time with this gentle man
and am grateful for his life!
Amen.

YOUR SAVING GRACE

Father,
As time passes and the span between death and life
    grows long,
I come to You with a grateful heart for Your grace in
    my pain.
As I look back since my beloved died,
I can see where You stepped in and made Your
    presence known.
When my emotions ran high or I was alone in
    despair,
You were right there by my side.

Though I know I can never go back,
I see now that my new life is a gift.
I will carry my love and memories of him forever in
    my heart.
And as I walk alone into the day,
I pray again that You will stay by my side
and continue to light my way.
Amen.

THE GIFT OF TEARS

Lord of joy and sorrow,
abundant tears flow freely
as I mourn for my beloved mate.

There are times when sweet memories bring silent
streams.
There are times when deep pain bursts forth in
wails.
There are even times when I don't know why I
weep.

All tears, I know now, are Your generous gift
of healing and release.
You know every tear I weep.
As I weep, grant those around me
Your gifts of understanding and compassion.

And so in love and sadness,
I accept Your gift of tears.
Let the tears flow like rivers of sorrow and of hope.
For I have faith that You will bless my weeping and
turn it into laughter.
Amen.

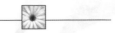

RECONCILIATION

Father of hope,
You have brought me to this place
on this long and difficult journey.
I know now that this journey never ends.
I have trusted You with my heart since the day my
     husband died.
In Your mercy, You have seen me through.

Lord, I come to You with a grateful heart.
In Your enduring time,
Your grace has softened the intensity of my pain.
And though I will always mourn his loss, I have
     survived.
I can now live more fully as I carry him in my heart.

In Your wisdom,
I have found new purpose to my life.
I place my faith in You
and know that You will continue to illuminate my
     way.

I entrusted You with my deepest pain,
and You answered my prayer.
Though my life is so different now,
I have found joy again.

You have shown me how to live moment to
    moment,
grace to grace.

So as I allow each new day to unfold before me,
I rest securely with the assurance of Your abiding
    love.
For I have walked through the dark valley
and live on to praise Your name.

Gracious, loving Lord, thank you for turning my
    mourning into joy.
Amen.

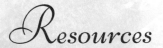

Resources

Websites
Center for Loss & Life Transition
www.centerforloss.com

WidowNet
www.fortnet.org/WidowNet

Magazines
Bereavement: A Magazine of Hope and Healing, 1-888-
604-4673, www.bereavementmag.com

Books
*A Decembered Grief: Living With Loss While Others Are
Celebrating*, by Harold Ivan Smith (Beacon Hill
Press, 1999).

*Getting Through the Night: Finding Your Way After the
Loss of a Loved One*, by Eugenie Price (Ballantine
Books, 1990).

Grieving the Loss of a Loved One, by Kathe Wunnenberg
(Zondervan, 2000).

How to Say Goodbye: Working Through Personal Grief, by
Joanne Smith and Judy Biggs (Aglow International,
1990).

Living When a Loved One Has Died, by Earl A. Grollman (Beacon Press, 1995).

The Oil of Joy for Mourning: 365 Daily Meditations to Comfort the Widowed, by Dr. Jan Sheble (Hendrickson Publishers, 1997).

Passage Through Grief: A Recovery Guide, by Barbara Baumgardner (Broadman & Holman Publishers, 1997).

Safe Passages: Words to Help the Grieving, by Molly Fumia (Conari Press, 2003).

Seasons of Grief and Healing, by James E. Miller (Augsburg Fortress Publishers, 2000).

Turn My Mourning Into Dancing, by Henri Nouwen (W Publishing Group, 2001).

National Support Groups

AARP Grief and Loss
601 E. St. NW
Washington, DC 20049
1-800-424-3410
www.aarp.org/griefandloss

Hope for Bereaved, Inc.
4500 Onondaga Blvd.
Syracuse, NY 13219
(315) 475-9675
www.hopeforbereaved.com

International THEOS (They Help Each Other Spiritually)
Foundation
322 Boulevard of the Allies, Suite 105
Pittsburgh, PA 15222-1919
(412) 471-7779

Parents Without Partners
1650 S. Dixie Hwy., Suite 510
Boca Raton, FL 33432
(561) 391-8833
www.parentswithoutpartners.org

Check with your parish or local telephone directory for Beginning Experience (a peer ministry for widowed, separated, or divorced parents and their children) and Rainbows (a program for helping children recover after experiencing loss resulting from death, divorce, or other life-altering crises).